THE MERMAID'S PURSE

Fleur Adcock was born in New Zealand in 1934. She spent the war years in England, returning with her family to New Zealand in 1947. She emigrated to Britain in 1963, working as a librarian in London until 1979. In 1977-78 she was writer-in-residence at Charlotte Mason College of Education, Ambleside. She was Northern Arts Literary Fellow in 1979-81, living in Newcastle, becoming a freelance writer after her return to London. She received an OBE in 1996, and the Queen's Gold Medal for Poetry in 2006 for *Poems 1960-2000* (Bloodaxe Books, 2000).

Fleur Adcock published three pamphlets with Bloodaxe: *Below Loughrigg* (1979), *Hotspur* (1986) and *Meeting the Comet* (1988), as well as her translations of medieval Latin lyrics, *The Virgin & the Nightingale* (1983). All her other collections were published by Oxford University Press until they shut down their poetry list in 1999, after which Bloodaxe published her collected poems, *Poems 1960-2000* (2000), followed by *Dragon Talk* (2010), *Glass Wings* (2013), *The Land Ballot* (2015), *Hoard* (2017) and *The Mermaid's Purse* (2021). *Poems 1960-2000* and *Hoard* are Poetry Book Society Special Commendations while *Glass Wings* is a Poetry Book Society Recommendation.

In October 2019 Fleur Adcock was presented with the New Zealand Prime Minister's Award for Literary Achievement in Poetry 2019 by the Rt Hon Jacinda Ardern.

FLEUR ADCOCK

The Mermaid's Purse

BLOODAXE BOOKS

ISBN: 978 1 78037 570 0

First published 2021 by
Bloodaxe Books Ltd,
Eastburn,
South Park,
Hexham,
Northumberland NE46 1BS

www.bloodaxebooks.com
For further information about Bloodaxe titles
please visit our website and join our mailing list
or write to the above address for a catalogue.

Supported using public funding by
**ARTS COUNCIL
ENGLAND**

Cover design: Neil Astley & Pamela Robertson-Pearce.

Printed in Great Britain by Bell & Bain Limited, Glasgow, Scotland, on
acid-free paper sourced from mills with FSC chain of custody certification.

ACKNOWLEDGEMENTS

Acknowledgements are due to the editors of the following publications in which some of these poems first appeared: *Long Poem Magazine, NZ Poetry Shelf, Pennine Platform, Poetry Review, Takahe, The Spectator,* and *The Times Literary Supplement.*

'Dead Poets' Society' was commissioned by *Magma* for its issue No 68, Summer 2017. 'Käthi Bowden in Bavaria' was commissioned by the Katherine Mansfield Society. 'The Other Christmas Poem' was commissioned by the Candlestick Press for *Christmas Spirit: Ten Poems to Warm the Heart.*

CONTENTS

POEMS FOR ROY
i.m. Roy Fisher, 1930-2017

The Mermaid's Purse

                      when you pick it up,
is full of squirmy sea-larvae –
she doesn't carry actual money,
but then she's not an actual mermaid
(actuality not being
a possible attribute of mermaids).

Three times I crossed the equator –
by water, that is; flying doesn't count.
The coloured surface is camouflage;
underneath is black; black and heaving.
Rats nest in the diver's helmet.
Why, then they must be sea-rats.

So where do we go from here? Down, down,
where the eels go. Don't wait for me –
I'll be along later. Down, down –
think of me supping at mermaid's milk
as you shrink into your philosophy.
The mermaid's child will be a dogfish.

Island Bay

Bright specks of neverlastingness
float at me out of the blue air,
perhaps constructed by my retina

which these days constructs so much else,
or by the air itself, the limpid sky,
the sea drenched in its turquoise liquors

like the paua shells we used to pick up
seventy years ago, two bays
along from here, under the whale's great jaw.

The Teacher's Wife

Braced on the landing stage in a gale
she will be waiting with her baby.
The ferry will be late, because of the weather.

It will thrash about offshore for a bit,
hurl a few packages at the beach,
and chug away without taking on passengers.

Phyllis and her brother will race up the hill
tripping over themselves with their story
about the teacher's wife – the teacher's wife –

who cried and threw her handbag in the sea.
Their mother will calm them down and tell them
never to speak about it again:

the teacher's wife, poor lady, can't help it.
She isn't used to the solitude here;
she's from the city…and, well…and, um…

But someone will speak about it. Gossip
will say what it hears. Gossip will joke:
'Just as well she didn't throw Fleur in the sea.'

Phyllis will write a story about it
eighty years later, and send it to Fleur,
in the nick of time; the very nick.

Fleur will explain about the dying father
on the other side of the Manukau Harbour
waiting to meet his first grandchild.

Let's have less talk of hysteria
by city people. There's plenty home-grown.
(And anyway, they were from Drury.)

*

Do you remember, asks the teacher's wife,
that woman who drowned herself at Grahams Beach?

No, mother, I was only just born,
if that. You'll have to tell me about it.

She walked into the sea, stood on a rock,
and hit herself on the head with a hammer

to knock herself out.
                    Well, that would do it –
(why are we laughing?) How do they know?

Did they find the hammer in her apron pocket
when she was washed up? Or was that someone else?

And don't call me the teacher's wife.

*

Almost irresistible, you'd think,
New Zealand being surrounded by these

emerald/sapphire/leaden waters
waiting to be entered, one way or another.

For example, there was that widowed
second cousin – I don't think we met her –

who slipped out of a care home in her nightie
and toddled across a road into the sea.

We call it the Shirley Brooks solution,
and cling to it for our own futures

(assuming one or other of us is fated
to be bunged into a bungalow facing a beach).

*

Naturally I think of Iris, walking
straight down Queen Street and into the harbour

(as soon as two boys had left the wharf),
her *'quite five cold struggling minutes'* before

she *'went deeply down once and again,
and breathed in water as if it were life, not death'.*

She felt her body roll slowly over,
with its face turned away from the sky:

*'peace: no green fields but just a green colour
and the sound of the waters, until they were dumb...'*

But suddenly came a rushing moment,
some sort of vehicle, the police matron...

*

All drowners fight at the end, they say.
No, at those moments close to the end.

At the end another urge takes over:
our brains have a sympathetic lobe

15

that yearns towards water, intoxicated
with the longing to be absorbed in it,

as if we'd spent our lives in denial
of the substance we're constructed from.

*

Have you noticed they're all women?
I could cite some men if necessary,

but we are the sea for men to drown in,
the ravening tide. No wonder we scare them.

*

Nothing could be easier, in Auckland
or indeed Wellington, than to cross a road
from the city centre and walk on to the wharf.

Green, green swilling under your feet;
seen through the cracks a deep green darkness
inviting you to step up and step down.

What could be easier
      what could be easier
nothing to stop you
      nothing to stop you;
nothing could be easier than
       nothing.

They'd fish you out, of course; the CCTV
(which was not a thing in the 1930s
for Iris) would have its fish-eye on you.

*

No such aqueous yearnings for the teacher's wife;
next time she finds herself aboard an ocean
it will be her care to keep an eye on Fleur

who is after all still a child, even
if she fancies herself as Juliet
and gazes too meltingly over the rail

(don't worry, mother: it's mostly fiction),
while in her sensible daytime mode
she's letting her father teach her to swim

between the strained and bulging canvas sides
of the pool erected on an upper deck
like an upside-down marquee full of water:

a capsule of Atlantic or Pacific
for the sea-deprived from post-war Britain
migrating to where seas are everywhere.

The Islands

Do I still long to go to the islands,
where the mosquitoes are the size of birds,
and rats chew your toothbrush while you're asleep?

Do I yearn for the soughing of palm-leaves
where ghosts are squatting on Bosini's grave?
Or should I leave all that to my children,

and their children, and their children's children? –
descendants of Bosini, every one;
products of my taste for the exotic.

A Bunch of Names

(for Greg)

Gregory Stuart Campbell. But first –
imagine it if you can – a time
before you had a name at all:
the days or weeks when you were 'the baby'
while we, your adamantine parents,
held out against each other's choices.

Your second name was easy: Stuart,
to commemorate your young uncle
killed in the war; but what could precede it?
Your father knew what he wanted; I
knew just as firmly what I didn't want.
How would we ever compromise?

I seem to remember a book of names,
each as impossible as the one before.
Reject, reject, reject, reject:
the rhythm was wrong, or the syllable count,
the associations, the sound of the vowels,
the lack of euphony with 'Campbell'.

We reached a settlement in the end:
Gregory. Nothing to do with a pope,
or Gregory Peck, or Gregorian chant –
just that neither of us hated it,
never having thought about it much.
It would do. This came as a surprise.

Meanwhile, your father had a vivid dream:
he saw you lying in your bassinet,
murmuring to yourself in the night:
'Stupid, clever, genius.'

He walked around repeating it
until I felt I had dreamed it myself.

Our genius child! Before too long
your Auntie Margaret, your lifelong fan,
coached you in your identity:
Gregory Stuart Campbell – or,
as she lovingly parroted after your own
version, 'Bebi Tuti Camel'.

At three you collected names of cars:
Hillman, Vanguard, Ford Popular,
Austin of England – I read them out,
you tucked them into your memory,
to dazzle friends and passers-by.
Your own name continued on its way.

Gregory evolved into Greg
(not easy for some of us). Then came
the mysteriously transferable Rocky,
interchangeable between brothers,
and, rather briefly in another context,
the now long obsolete Snookums.

The soubriquet that charmed me most
is the one I first heard Lily use
to your new grandchild: 'Go to Pops!'
It's been a long journey for you,
but secretly inside my head
you never stop being 'my darling boy'.

The Fur Line

When I was working in the factory,
stitching open-ended zip fasteners
at one of a row of sewing machines,
someone brought in some kittens in a box.

I didn't wait to consult my husband;
I travelled home on the tram after work
with Jonathan snuggled in my bosom.
We had a cat before we had a child.

Sally and Midge, Pussywillow, Ada:
all that fluff got into our synapses,
transmitting itself down generations,
from nerve to nerve, or however it works.

Tiger and Snowflake, Marigold and Prince...
too late to say I've gone off predators
in favour of protecting the birdlife,
when I've bred a tribe of ailurophiles.

It's out of my hands; this is the future:
Brucie, Melba, Sasha, Lady Gaga.
It's no surprise that my great-granddaughters
grow up co-sleeping with their mothers' cats.

A Feline Forage in Auckland

Prince butts in through the cat flap
with a small dark whirligig
that whizzes on the floor like a top:
a bumblebee, you'd think it was.

Not so: when I brace to pick it up
it turns into a cicada.
I set off on a rescue trip
with an empty saucepan full of buzz.

An hour later another scrap
of biodiversity's brought in.
Lopped of the tail it had to drop
it slinks reptilianly away

in the direction of under the sink;
and it's – what do you think? A skink.

House

There was the tiepin-sized guitar
sealed into a shallow indentation
in a bedroom floorboard, as a tease,
forever floating in translucent varnish.

There was the pohutukawa by the gate
planted over the umbilical cord
of the daughter now in her twenties.

There was the patchwork timber floor
constructed out of several smaller floors
(wash-house, lavatory, entry step –
ancient kauri, the lot of them,
and all the levels coordinated)
in that corner of the kitchen
where the sun sets behind high trees.

There was the sunset. There was the view.
There was the horizon of extinct volcanoes.

And then they all melted into money.

Peter's Hat

(for Peter Bland)

Seeing you there, Peter, on the cover
of *broadsheet/19* (your tribute issue),
looking very northern under your hat,
I realise, good God, we're 83
and I've never written you a poem.

Could it be that I took you for granted,
my trans-hemispheric wandering friend?
Every now and then we'd happen to be
both in the same country at the same time,
but it tended not to last very long.

No sooner would you seem to be settled
than you'd get the urge to pack up and move on.
'Well, I've put my house on the market,' you'd
say, having rung the shipping company
(to be greeted as their pet customer).

House after house – glorious, some of them –
heartlessly cleared and vacated and sold
because it had suddenly dawned on you,
probably in the middle of the night,
you and Beryl were in the WRONG COUNTRY.

Looking back, you've told me, you feel guilty
about what you put her through. Don't worry;
I'm sure she forgave you; it was simply
the way you are: home is where your hat is
(which I was sorry to hear you've now lost –

although the replacement looks much the same).

A Small Correction

(i.m. Mike Doyle)

It was a brown coat, Mike, not a blue one
I was wearing when you first caught sight of me,
Alistair's wife, in Philosophy I;
the only coat I owned that year was brown.

Blue was the colour of your little Austin,
at the sight of which, pulling up outside,
Alistair would prepare his excuses,
leaving you to confide again in me

about whatever it was this time:
your dying wife, your platonic ardour
for the one who would be next, or just exactly
how guilty that ought to make you feel.

Gentle, apologetic, vaguely awkward,
good-looking enough to pose in a full page ad
for a tailoring firm, decked out in paper hat
and streamers: I hope they let you keep the suit.

In the Cupboard

Still sneezing from the dust, I uncover
among the souvenir shell necklaces
and the pottery beads from Kathmandu

an oblong satin-lined box cherishing
the pendant I begged my parents to buy
in Queenstown: three ovals of fake amber
lined up along a wispy chain.

The resin, discoloured now, makes the flowers
amazingly suspended inside
harder to distinguish – unless the petals
have themselves been leached of their colours.

What's next? In a cellophane packet, five
diamante and fake pearl buttons
from my wedding dress (not my choice,
either the buttons or the dress itself).

Also a teardrop pearl on a thin gold chain,
the gift of someone who thought, years too late,
that this was the kind of thing I might like.

Giza

(for Cait)

It was in this dress – pink and apricot
glazed cotton in a geometric print
with a draw-string waist, boat neck, small cap sleeves
(home-made from a Simplicity pattern –

we all made our own dresses in those days) –
that I rode a camel in the desert
outside Cairo to the Great Pyramid
of Giza. (Less intrepid than it sounds:

a tourist guide was holding the bridle.)
The skirt was knee-length, and rather too tight –
not suitable for an Arab country;
it rucked right up as I clambered aboard.

Then – a bit of a surprise to me – rain
began to fall. (This was February
1963 – that famous winter.)
Anyway, I thought you might like the dress.

Siena

In retrospect it had been a good move
to fall out with the bibliographer,
(to whom I'd had to explain the bidet
in our room), and catch the train on my own.
I found myself seven centuries back,
in a mirage with a striped cathedral.

On the second night I was picked up by
Antonio, a medical student,
who cruised outside the Pinacoteca
on patrol for arty foreign women.

He took me up to a battered castle,
accommodatingly provided with
unlit architecture to lean into.
We kept in touch by letters for a year.

Realms

Much have I travelled in the realms of gold...
mostly in books, but also in the more
gilded provinces of, while it lasted,
youth, or the willing suspension – heigh-ho,
that willing suspension – assisted by
less than explicit electric lighting.

I refer you to a certain café
notable for the bubble-wrap effect
that cast a golden veil over my eyes –
either an epiretinal membrane
or something we'd pulled down around ourselves
for protection in tumultuous times.

Or was it that fine mesh Vulcan crafted,
smith-work of the slenderest calibre,
to entrap his wife with her fancy man?
Not much good came of that, as I recall,
except the amusement it provided
for the spectators. I'm saying nothing.

In the Cloud

There is flirting
and there is Fleurest;
there is the sweet bye-and-bye
and the sweet never-was,
and a Vera Lynn song over
the white cliffs of nowhere.

Hollyhocks

The hollyhocks at my door needn't have bothered
flaring out in a whirl of roseate skirts.
My guest has been – let's hope the right word is 'delayed'.

Yet still I carry on preparing for her stay:
scrubbing and scouring, smoothing what's already smooth,
primping, prettifying, tweaking; scrubbing some more.

Berries

Spindleberries; you can't eat them.
That gaudy rig is for entertainment.

Outside the camp is *terra ignota*.

Tell me the names of some berries:
what are whortleberries? Can you eat them?

Esurient; etiolated. We have hunger.

Tell me the names of some berries.
Blueberries, colour-berries; black you can eat.
Outside the camp it's... not that kind of jungle.
If it had snakes we'd lure them to our *cucina*.

Those teenage children have lighted on a morsel
and are sharing it between them like the host.
It won't save them – not now.
Last week, maybe; even yesterday; not now.

Mulberry, rowanberry, elderberry.

Outside the camp she is surrounded by briars:
la Belle au Bois Dormant.
Not that kind of jungle. Rosehips might save her,
but not the thorns. The dog rose will bite her.

I am pierced by a needle. By a spindle. Beware.

Those children squatting by the roadside
are picking maggots out of a thing they've found.

In the prison camp in Indonesia
he used to eat flies. He told me.

Amazing Grace

Someone is bawling 'Amazing Grace'
from the vault below St Mary Woolnoth.

It's John Newton, the hymn writer,
reformed slave trader, famous convert,

'once an infidel and libertine...
Rector of these united parishes',

whose mortal remains are deposited,
says the marble tablet, below this church.

But St Mary Woolnoth sold the crypt
to the City and South London Railway.

John Newton, the former incumbent,
is not recumbent under the floor

in the ticket hall of Bank Station,
confused vibrations rattling his coffin.

He's been translated to a better place;
admirers requisitioned his bones

and shipped them back, with Mrs Newton's,
to his old parish of Olney, Bucks.

In which case why is he here, bellowing
from somewhere sepulchral about grace?

If it's grace he wants there's Hawksmoor's ceiling
with its pretty fanlights (buy a postcard).

No, that won't do; that's frivolity.
It's souls he wants, not architecture;

he's here to free them from their snares,
and he's not the kind of man you can shut up.

His mission is to strike the shackles
from the ankles of the City traders

and other worshippers of Mammon –
slaves to flummery, slaves to pelf.

More slaves here than in Olney;
even within earshot, slaves galore.

Käthi Bowden in Bavaria

Käthi is good at looking enigmatic,
but Frau Fischer is not to be discouraged:
'Ah, that is so strange about you English!
You don't enjoy discussing your complaints.'

What is strange about this German spa town
is that it possesses a gully
just like the one in Käthi's Thorndon,
and a harbour, what's more. Käthi is a tease.

Fräulein Sonia and the Herr Professor
have gone off to examine the modern soul.
The Baron is receiving due deference.
The servants are muttering in the kitchen.

Käthi is pleased to have studied German.
They have all found their way into her notes –
the maids, the postman, the posturing guests,
the Advanced Lady, the anxious father –

to be subtly altered, as she alters herself…
But a surge of delegates is approaching,
about to be greeted by the Mayor
in yet another commemoration.

This is a different century.
Käthi slips around the corner,
tucking her notebook into her muff.
If she is quick enough she may dodge them.

Divining

What you do, he said,
to make divining-rods:
take a metal coat-hanger, like this,
and pliers; clip it into an L-shape –
you won't need the bit with the hook;
bend the angle to 90°.
Make another one the same: two L-shapes,
one for each hand, matching.

Right: the long side is the divining-rod,
the short side is the handle.
Curl your fist round it – loose like this –
softly; no pressure;
looser: you're holding a baby bird,
it's timid, it needs to breathe.

Now: one step at a time
steady as you can, slowly, slowly,
glide forward, both rods parallel,
pointing ahead, level with the ground.
No, no; don't clutch – let them flutter
when they want to. Not everyone can do it.

The first time I tried, he said,
I was visiting an infants' school:
rows of little kids cross-legged on the floor.
A teacher was giving a demonstration
and she let me have a go.
When the rods are aware of water
they swing slowly towards each other
and cross over. It's a powerful sensation,
like living things writhing in your hands.

We took turns walking round the hall,
divining the radiators for a start –
you couldn't fail to notice it.

And of course people are just bags of water;
all those kids down at knee-level
triggered the divining-rods –
got them criss-crossing as I walked through.
There I was with these wire antennae
flexing and flipping over all the little heads.

Welsh

If all else fails you could learn Welsh:
such an exacting discipline –

surely they'd have faith in you then?
I've heard of good online tutors.

Tip-top health is not essential
if you remain articulate

and your fingers still obey you,
whatever else may be astray.

A person who has mastered Welsh,
or grasped more than the fringe of it,

is not to be dismissed lightly.
What an example to us all! –

except of course to Welsh people,
who have an unfair advantage.

Yes, it could well be the answer:
Welsh. Or perhaps hieroglyphics.

This Fountain

Hats are all very well, but the best shade
is an umbrella of leaves, high up, to
sit under catching words from passers-by –

'But then what if you're making a salad;
do you wash it in bottled water? Or
what do you do?' And they move out of range.

I amble along the path. 'This fountain
is being repaired and has been turned off.'
(Like the sky, you could say, these last long weeks.)

The stone receptacle built into the base
for dogs to drink water from is empty –
or was, until a family arrived

with anxious children and relief supplies.
That's the dogs attended to, just for now.
When is the sky going to be repaired?

Tiny flies position themselves under
my hat brim and dance in front of my eyes,
trying to drink the moisture from my breath.

Magnolia Seed Pods

Among the wonders vouchsafed to me
during my suburban wanderings
in two countries, this one and that one,

were these exotic excrescences,
each a miniature pineapple,
framed in petals the size of saucers.

The first I saw were strewn underfoot,
with no magnolia bloom in sight:
a mystification until I asked.

It was late in life when I found them.
Who would have thought I'd still be allowed
to walk out freely where there were trees

and carry on as I've always done:
picking things up and looking at them?

Bats

Once again the low scoop over my shoulder
by the lilacs, the dipped-wing fly-past,
the reversal in mid-thought, the sudden soar; but

imagined this time, and always something else:
a late-flying bird, a wavering twig,
a trick of the eyesight at dusk.

Scoop, swoop, loop the loop.

Your small elderly faces, gaping

If I could but see

Spooks

Again and again, and never again,
Spooks

Beloved.

*   *

That particular area of sky,
in the lee of the bulkiest sycamore
(because you don't like the wind)

waits for your entry on to the scene,
your merry aerial patterns against
the post-sunset – a greenish-yellow backdrop.

Look at all the insects
my foliage has bred for you,
if you would only come back.

I can't eat them myself;
the foxes don't want them.
No one but you can dance after them.

*   *

You were established; you were a colony
for a dozen years or more before the crash –

a colony of one, to begin with,
strayed here from some wood or other

straining our credulity –
no one else around here had bats.

And then, *mirabile dictu*, you were
plural, truly, whenever I counted.

Flittermouse; flattermouse –
I felt so honoured to have bats.

Better than television,
all those evenings, in the long dusk –

Come and look, visitors;
grandchildren, kneel at the window –

until a derelict bird box, forgotten
for years, crashed out of my tallest tree.

You know the one about the Bluebird of Happiness –
all the time in your own backyard?

*   *

Gone, stuck in the past, blocked.
Gone beyond the back of beyond,
back of the rainbow, back of the black stump.

This new scientifically designed
National Trust approved bat box
won't lure you back. You won't see it.

You liked the old one, mounded with droppings,
rotting away from whatever clamped
its crumbling panels fast to the tree.

Let me prevail on you to relent –
wherever you are, and whichever wood,
Coldfall or Highgate, has received you

If you're alive.

Come and spook me; come and dazzle me
with your darkness when I least expect you,
early on a May morning or at sunset,

zooming out into your high patrol.
When I'm finally convinced you're over,
strike me senseless with astonishment.

Novice Flyer

What was the use of these brisk new wing-blades
or these legs like springy twigs, young robin,
if they couldn't lift you just a bit higher
than the jaws that snatched and punctured you
and then dropped you on my flower bed,
right here, beside the antirrhinums?

It's far too early for a rosy breast,
but I see the advance markers of it:
two shreds of orange fluff on your bosom,
nestled among the tweedy russet.

You loll on my hand as I pick you up,
surprisingly heavy, surprisingly warm –
just getting the knack of being dead.
The reddest thing is the splash on my palm.

Wood Mice

They'd better stop doing that, though,
if they want to go on living here –
running up the stairs in kangaroo hops
(a big leap for mouse-kind),

nibbling at everything from stationery
to paracetamol, shinning up
the striped ladder of the tradescantia
to chew on its translucent stem-joints

as if they were celery (the cheek of it)
and playing hide and seek under the bureau;
then galloping down again, a sight to see,
their little bandy legs viewed from behind –

otherwise it's into a box with them –
a humane one, of course –
and down to the woods for a new life;
but it has been known to go wrong,

alas, O alas,
which tends to make the householder
more sentimental
than might otherwise be.

So in the meantime, pending reform,
a discreet crumble of toast
or a few peanuts under the cooker
for Big-ears in the night.

Sparrowhawk

That day Storm Ciara brought a sparrowhawk
to hunch on my wind-wobbled buddleia
dazzling me with her brown and white barred front,
the stripiest thing since Bridget Riley.

She sat full on, a witch from the woodlands,
immobile apart from her swivel-head,
trying to cast the evil eye on me
through the glass of my dining-room window.

Her gold-ringed orbs were hypnotic, all right;
the small birds had deserted their feeders.
I quaked for them, and for our battered globe.
It took days until my robin dared come
to chat with me in his throaty subsong,
before the next weekend and Storm Dennis.

Election 1945

The first election I can remember
is the one in which my father and mother
voted Winston Churchill out of office,
and we got the National Health Service –

which gave me an exaggerated view
of what democracy can actually do.

The Little Theatre Club

1945: the Principal Boy
(Ninette, *née* Edith, seventy this year)
hauls out her costume trunk again: it's time
to shroud her bony shanks in the green tights
that have served her well since before the war.

Now there's no blackout more children will come
to watch this thing they'll call a 'pantomine'.
No, they won't think of it as magical;
it can't out-magic *The Wizard of Oz*
or other films they've seen at the Regal.

But they'll cotton on to the convention
of gender-swapping, loving its daftness
(who's the Dame? It will have to be Anton,
Ninette's husband, parading his bosom),
and they'll giggle at the grown-ups having fun.

And what will you remember, my young dears?
Will it be the lights, the smell of make-up,
the topical jokes about coal rationing
and Mr Attlee? It will be those tights:
apple-green, and wrinkled about the knees.

The Other Christmas Poem

Or you might prefer to read about the Christmas
when after all the hosting and feasting

we finally got the kids off to bed
and the rest of us, the grown-ups
(if that's an accurate designation),

opened up another case of wine
and put on some Rolling Stones records.

I think it was Ruth, a friend of a friend,
who found the room a bit overheated
and made the decision to take her top off –

something it seemed she was given to doing
at the slightest provocation.

Her husband greeted this with tolerance,
and before too long had removed his shirt;
several other people shed theirs.

One of the women undid her dress,
with a vaguely absent-minded air.

The dancing hotted up; Ruth took off her bra;
someone stepped casually out of his trousers.
You can see the way this is going.

By the time Alex tiptoed upstairs
for more wine from the stash in his study

(the children, thank God, were sleeping soundly)
he was the only adult in the house
wearing so much as his underpants.

Ah, what a memorable party,
we'd reminisce in the years that followed,

thinking of the camaraderie –
and of how our necks had been stiff with the strain
of never glancing below anyone's waist.

Anadyomene

Talking about Greek words reminds me:
if you were to strip off the layers
of emulsion on that stretch of wall
beside the window in the spare bedroom

you might find microscopic flecks
of golden paint: traces, you could say,
of the tresses of Botticelli's Venus,
copied studiously from a postcard
a teenage fan bought at the Uffizi.
It was all an education to him.

After a year or two, he rollered over her.
The magazine shot of Liza Minnelli
(with clothes on) inside his wardrobe door
survived his occupation of the room.

Victoria Road

I'm saying to Meg and Alex
'I came past your street this afternoon.
I wanted to visit you but you're dead.'
And Meg is saying, in her sensible way,
'Can't be helped. Next time check up first',

while Alex gives a sort of rueful smile
mouthing 'Sorry!' as if through a window
(I can't hear him), and flinging his hands out
in apology, as when they met me
at Kathmandu airport in a thunderstorm:
'Sorry about the rain!'

Sorry about the deaths. But let's not start.

Anyway, now that we've established that
we can get on with the conversation.
I'll show them the pictures I took
of Meg beside the two saplings
on a riverside walk in Stony Stratford
where we planted Alex's ashes;
we used to visit the swans around there.

Alex will embark on a story
about spotting his hero Graham Greene
in the south of France, and trying
to pluck up courage…
I think I may have heard it before,
but I was never sure of the ending.

To Stephenie at 11 PM

One last crumb of family history,
dear cousin, all these months after your death:
our great-grandmother Martha used to say
'Night brings home all sorrows.' So I find it.

Lightning Conductor

On the eighteenth anniversary of
my mother's death, I've been watching a man
in a vertiginous cherry-picker

attaching copper wire to the finials
on the church roof. I'm pleased with myself
for remembering the word 'finial',

which I associate with a poem
by Amy Clampitt, but madly searching
for the name of my mother's neighbour

who kindly let me lodge in her house
on one of my visits to Wellington.
When I was leaving it for the airport

the taxi, swinging around two corners,
startled me with a glimpse of my mother,
to whom I'd already said goodbye,

walking firmly and with concentration
in her familiar red dressing gown
up the outside staircase to her flat.

It was not my last view of her,
but the last on that particular trip,
and likely to outlive several others.

Finial. It sounds like a fancy,
over-decorated word for 'final'.
Lightning is the least of my worries.

The Annual Party

They have wheeled in the famous novelist,
the sacred monster; we thought he was dead,
after that biography... We saunter past
his chariot, pretending not to look.

In fact we are rather more concerned
with the actual dead whose obituaries
we've read – or written – during the year
(less wittily than they'd have written ours),

or with the barely living but absent.
We can point to the spot in this very room
where we last tried to find encouraging
words for our friend who had heard them all.

Then there are the inexplicably
missing (has anyone recent news
of that not-always-patient editor?
Has his workload finally crushed him?)

– And of course the explicably missing:
the poet who for as long as his term
on the Council lasted felt it his duty
to show his face here, but shows it no more,

and the older poet confined to views
of the bird-feeders outside his windows
or, when his carers turn him around,
of the bleak peaks he refuses to leave –

unlike his near contemporary
from a gentler brand of rural landscape
who trotted about with her little trolley
year after year until – when was the last time?

Instead we find ourselves among
a sprinkling of the pseudo-senior –
writing for *The Oldie* at 53
(bah! We've got children older than that) –

and a phalanx of the under-40s,
lured in by the new initiative
(we know what that was all about). Well,
just one more circuit of the room, perhaps.

Letting Them Know

(for Connie Bensley)

We need to find a way of telling them,
those of us addicted to living alone;

if we lose the power of speech, and all the rest,
we need a non-vocal way to make it known:

not to call for help – it's too late for that –
but simply to inform them that the bird has flown.

No particular advantage is gained
by having someone there on the spot

when all you need is a messenger
to convey the information, posthumous or not;

you could leave the front door open, perhaps,
for some passerby to figure out the plot.

The thing is – how can we put this gently? –
we just want to be found before we rot.

Blackberries

1

Soft with last Thursday's deluge, blackberries
melt into my hands as I pick them.
My polythene bag oozes, catching
on bramble thorns. This is the best place,
this boggy, shaggy heath-in-the-making
neglected behind the tennis-courts.

2

An old man pads along on his son's arm.
I overtake them, to check the profile
of my probable contemporary
between the cloth cap and the jacket collar
in case it belongs to an acquaintance:
grey moustache, drooping underlip… No.

3

'Have you got the time?' 'Sorry, what?' 'The time!' –
a lad practising basketball shots.
Avoiding my sleeve, I tilt my watch-face
with one sticky, garnet-stained finger.
'Six o'clock.' The park is emptying.
I have a watch. He has the time.

Tatters

A wind from all directions
is harrying fits and scraps of snow
as I scramble out of bed
to look up the origins
of the word 'tatterdemalion'.

I wonder if Shakespeare made it up.
But no: it's post-Shakespearean,
1622 and later –
derived from 'tatter' or 'tattered',
with a 'factitious element'.

Clearly somebody made it up,
and other jokers fiddled with it.
It can have a double 'l' –
Tatterdemallion. Rhymes with Italian.
Or so they say.

And look – wouldn't you know –
someone has named a band after it.
Meanwhile the snow... Also the wind...
It feels pretty Shakespearean to me.
I bet he knew it anyway –

even if it isn't in a play.

The Old Road

I meet some sheep and pause to laugh at them.
They stare at me and turn to each other:
'What does she mean?' they ask. 'What does she mean?'

I mean them no harm: I'm bubbling over
with goodwill. I've come here empty-handed,
but I can see the funny side of sheep.

A hand-painted sign: 'Caution. Nesting birds.'
Lapwings, probably, or curlews. The sheep
with their risky hooves are across the road,

on the downward slope, towards the river,
behind a gate. There's been some thought in this:
no offspring are going to be trampled.

Ah, I can guess where all this is heading:
the nature notes, the forced optimism,
the upland landscape with its bleakish tinge,

even these kingcups blazing with light in
the ditch, and a lapwing clattering up
into the sky. Don't tell me. Don't tell me.

POEMS FOR ROY

i.m. Roy Fisher, 1930-2017

Dead Poets' Society

Yet once more, O ye laurels, and once more,
myrtles and suchlike, I come to complain –
though not to you, innocent shrubs. My target
is mouldy old Death, who keeps grabbing my friends.
I have some words for you, Skeletonguts:
You've snatched more than your share of poets,
crammed them in your long pack and carried them off
to munch at leisure in your den.
Why couldn't you have used some judgement?
To you we may all seem much the same,
but I tell you, Boneface, today
the life you had the gall to pluck
(not untimely – he was old enough,
but gifted with wits, with wit, with a brain
that these witless times can't easily spare)
was exceptional. It was Roy you took.
Think about that, if you can, for a moment,
Gogglesockets, and repent!
Yes, Roy, dear friend and matchless poet;
Roy, who has not left his peer.
He and I kept a running correspondence
to note each colleague who became your prey –
endless mailings headed 'Another one'.
We were against you, as he managed to say
to your face when you came fumbling for him.
His last word, I'm proud to report, was 'Fuck'.

Jade Plant

This one's called *The Pathetic Fallacy*:
The 'money tree' you gave me in the form of

a bulbous, finger-length twig to bring home
on the train in a margarine container,

pot up in gritty compost, and watch
expanding through slow reliable decades,

has spent these last few weeks bending over,
limb by stiff limb, trunk turning pliable,

fat green oval jade coins dropping off
in twiggy clusters of three and four

as if it 'knew something'; as if
(what nonsense) it had 'decided' to die.

Do not resuscitate, you said once
in another context. I shan't.

Double Haiku

On the other hand
choosing the spring equinox
as a date to be

blighted for ever
could have been called irony,
if you had chosen.

Elm

As I stumble around among
words like 'outlive' and 'survivor'
in connection with the grand elm
just up the lane from your house – or
your former house, as it is now –
in the Peak District (too high up,
you said, for the elm bark beetle)
the scenario's clear enough.

When I allow myself to plunge
into my file of your letters
from our pre-electronic days
and your annual birthday cards,
each one inscribed with a poem,
it won't surprise me if I find
(secreted where I can't lose it)
a cellophane pack of pressed leaves.

Four Poems and a Funeral

I've kept this red rubber band;
it's the one I took off

the flowers from my garden –
wallflowers, drooping lilac

(you know how cut lilac droops),
forget-me-nots, rosemary –

before I laid them down
on your wicker coffin.

Maundy Thursday 2017

The priest, no longer a young man, creaks down
on to his knees, washes and dries my foot,
wrenches himself upright with his stick, and
moves on to the next prewashed foot.

Listen: those must be the hosts of heaven;
why else would they be singing in Latin?
They are Nick and Marian and the rest
up in the choir gallery. Same thing.

Incense. Candles. Hymns, for God's sake!
How you would have hated all this;
and how you despised your younger self
for having once fallen for it.

One day in a church in Romania
you caught me trying the elaborate
hand gestures of the Orthodox blessing,
so much fancier than the Roman one.

I was copying a peasant woman.
I was, I have to admit, showing off.
But to whom? To her? To God? Not to you.
Your face was without any expression,

yet you were always tolerant of me,
with my role-play and my little dramas,
enmired in my fallen state. There are
friends, you said, and there are intimates.

The priest kissed my foot; it was his duty.
I thought how they wash the feet of the dead.
I thought of your feet yesterday, under
your coffin lid, and now nowhere at all.

An April Bat

From the place where you are now
you've sent me a bat. Thank you.
I looked out of the pantry window
to catch a glimpse of the sunset

(rosy-pink with pollution as it was)
and there, circling and flipping low
above my flowering trees,
apple and lilac, was this bat.

Birds, we used to send each other:
a woodpecker, a jay. But this
is for the dark time.
Don't think I value it less

for being a cliché. You know
I haven't a very original mind.
You were generous enough
to send me a thing I'd understand.

Porridge

I was thinking about that saucepan of yours:
the Pyrex one, so improbable, made of
amber glass, the colour of barley sugar.

Not a utensil to be used on gas, I
imagined; but on your electric cooker
it squatted contentedly in its glory.

Everything about it looked precarious –
liable to melt into golden syrup
as soon as it encountered heat, or explode

into a shrapnel blitz of orange splinters.
But of course it was tougher than that: solid,
quaint with survival from an earlier age.

All you had to do was not drop it too hard.
I almost felt I was demeaning it by
stirring mere porridge in it. But oh, the glow!

Now that the house is cleared it must be somewhere –
safe in a crate, perhaps, or a cardboard box –
until whatever happens to it happens.

Annual Tribute

I needn't think that just because you're dead
I'm absolved from my annual duty
of writing a poem for your birthday;

it's just that this one won't come on a card
like its predecessors in our sequence
of reciprocal yearly well-wishings.

In the old days it might have reflected
on the weather, or something topical –
your latest book of poems, your new cat –

or some mathematical property
of your age: 'tetrahedral' went down well
on your eighty-fourth (a magic number).

Usually we tried to be funny.
This year there's an election to gawp at;
plenty of scope there for satire, ho, ho.

Also, being greetings card doggerel,
it had to rhyme. You had a knack for that.
One year you wrote a virtuoso riff

circling around without ever naming
a rude word I'd used when playing Scrabble
with friends who were slightly prim (that's a clue).

All those ditties fluttering between us!
I'm sure I can come up with another;
it's just rather tricky to gauge the tone

in this new situation. Still, here goes,
even if I can't expect a response
on my own birthday, or ever again

(unless you've prepared a massive surprise);
even if – yes, I know the 'even ifs'.
I'd better think of a joke to end with.

Winter Solstice

Nine months on from the spring equinox
when that 'Are you sitting down?' phone call
implanted the unshiftable fact.

Nine months, as if it were a full term
pregnancy, with a birth almost due.
But what shall I hug to my bosom

when the time comes? All I can predict
will be something small, dark and smothered:
a lump of knowledge, wrapped in a shawl.

Snowman

You were my snow contact, my on-the-phone
link to a vicarious fairyland.
'Are you snowed in?' I'd ask. Yes, you'd confirm,
as the Tesco van got stuck in the lane
again on its stoic route from Buxton.
'Ah!' – (trying to make my sigh of envy
sound a bit more like sympathy) – 'Oh dear.
Just boring old rain down here.' That was then.

Now that London has managed a blizzard
and what it brings – the hypnotic light, the
self-important coping with frozen pipes –
I've no one in the Peak District to tell.
On my lawn a blackbird is peck-shredding
the orange-peel grin from next door's snowman.

Mayonnaise

'Could I prevail upon you', said Lorna,
'to make me some more of that mayonnaise?' –
with garlic, for dipping *crudités* in:
a small thank-you-for-having-me gesture
after my stay in her Newcastle house.

She had another guest on my last night.
He sat with us next morning at breakfast,
drinking his coffee as I stirred and whisked
and added this or that and whisked some more,
while Lorna made notes. He said there should be

a genre painting recording the scene
(this being in the days before Facebook)
in case the three of us became famous,
called 'Roy Fisher watching Lorna Tracy
watching Fleur Adcock making mayonnaise.'

Quite soon he dropped me off at the station,
and drove to Durham for his assignment.
'A most entertaining man, Roy', I wrote
in my journal on the train going home,
'with a nice line in pedantic phrases.'

He was fifty-two, which I then supposed
to be quite old, but as it came about
we had something like thirty-five years more,
on and off, to entertain each other
one way or the next, as our lives allowed.

NOTES

The Teacher's Wife (13)

In May 2013 I was signing books after a reading in Auckland when a woman asked me to sign one for a 90-year-old relative, Phyllis, who had been my father's star pupil when he was teaching in a tiny, one-teacher school at Grahams Beach on the Manukau Harbour, a place then scarcely accessible except by boat. During his second year there, 1934, I was born and my mother's father entered his final illness. She took me across the harbour to visit him before his death, but her first attempt to do so was thwarted in a dramatic way. I learned this from a little story Phyllis sent me about an episode in her childhood that had puzzled her; fortunately there was just time for me to explain it to her before she died. I began this poem in February 2017, struck by the contrast between Phyllis's account of the incident at Grahams Beach and my mother's reminiscences of her time there. It grew into a wider meditation on ways in which New Zealand women, including Iris Wilkinson (the poet and novelist Robin Hyde), have been drawn to the sea or to drowning. It became an excuse for playing games with tenses, registers and viewpoints. I refer to myself in the third person – as a baby, as a teenager on board ship – and to my mother (who in her confused old age sometimes thought me a contemporary) under a stylised label. I hope she'd have forgiven me.

Käthi Bowden in Bavaria (35)

In 1909 Katherine Mansfield was hiding out in Wörishofen, Bavaria, because she was pregnant and had run away from her husband George Bowden, not the father of the child, after one night. The pregnancy came to nothing, but she began writing the stories that eventually made up her first collection, *In a German Pension*. She based several of the German characters on people she had known in Wellington, and the landscape also underwent confusing changes in her imagination.

Bats (41)

They responded: the following year (2019), to my astonishment, they or another pair of bats moved into the new NT bat box. But the miracle was too good to last, and before too long they disappeared one by one, perhaps the victims of predators. My appeal for their return must stand.